How *The Lion King* Made It to the Stage

Nancy Capaccio

Cavendish Square

New York

Published in 2019 by Cavendish Square Publishing, LLC
243 5th Avenue, Suite 136, New York, NY 10016

Copyright © 2019 by Cavendish Square Publishing, LLC

First Edition

Library of Congress Cataloging-in-Publication Data

Names: Capaccio, Nancy.
Title: How the Lion King made it to the stage / Nancy Capaccio.
Description: First edition. | New York : Cavendish Square, 2018. | Series: Getting to Broadway | Includes bibliographical references and index.
Identifiers: LCCN 2017054201 (print) | LCCN 2017055326 (ebook) | ISBN 9781502635099 (ebook) | ISBN 9781502635082 (library bound) | ISBN 9781502635105 (pbk.)
Subjects: LCSH: John, Elton. Lion King (Musical)--Juvenile literature.
Classification: LCC ML410.J64 (ebook) | LCC ML410.J64 C35 2018 (print) | DDC 792.6/42--dc23
LC record available at https://lccn.loc.gov/2017054201

Editorial Director: David McNamara
Editor: Tracey Maciejewski
Copy Editor: Rebecca Rohan
Associate Art Director: Amy Greenan
Designer: Lindsey Auten
Production Coordinator: Karol Szymczuk
Photo Research: J8 Media

Printed in the United States of America

Contents

WALT DISNEY PICTURES
PRESENTS
THE LION KING
Soundtrack Available on Cassette and Compact Disc From
Walt Disney Records
STARTS FRIDAY, JUNE 24 AT THEATRES EVERYWHERE

The Animated Movie

The story of how the musical *The Lion King* made it to the stage is as exciting, dramatic, and unique as the show itself. The musical would require an all-new union of artistry and commercialism. The journey entailed breathtaking risks and yielded equally breathtaking rewards. The events that happened along the way encompass many of the themes of the musical: aspirations, challenges, support, and community.

At its heart, theater is about artists who enjoy bringing to life stories that the audience relishes experiencing. There is a third "player," which is made up of the organizations that have the financial resources and the drive to make professional theater happen. Nowhere is that equation more clear than on Broadway, where mounting a musical costs millions of dollars.

Opposite: This poster, painted by John Alvin, helped create *The Lion King*'s memorable brand.

When telling the story of how *The Lion King* made it to the stage, we're going to look at the artistic challenges as well as the fascinating and high-risk business side. We'll also explore how a simple interest in lions and hyenas first turned into a blockbuster movie and then into a groundbreaking musical amassing more than $6 billion in box-office sales. That dollar figure is far greater than movie blockbusters such as *Titanic, Avatar,* or any single *Harry Potter* or *Star Wars* movie. And we'll top it off with how *The Lion King* is still growing, twenty years later.

The Origins

If Mufasa, the lion king, could look back on his beginnings, he might break into a chuckle. His wife, Queen Sarabi, might tease him by saying, "You've come a long way, baby!"

This coming-of-age animated movie—about how a lion cub would grow up and need to take his father's place—did not start out that way. Not by a long shot. While this was Walt Disney Pictures' thirty-second full-length animated film, it was the studio's first to be based on an original story. Writing a brand-new story for a movie was the first of many risks that Disney was willing to take. Creating a winning story from scratch is not easy, especially with Disney's intention of offering movies that work on different levels, so that both children and their parents can enjoy the story. This strategy is part of what makes Disney so successful.

Surprisingly, this charming movie began in 1988 as somewhat of a documentary inspired by a National Geographic feature about lions and hyenas in Africa. While in development, the treatment was originally called "King of the Kalahari," then "King of the Beasts," and later "King of the Jungle." At that point, somebody pointed out that lions don't actually live in the jungle. The development team nixed the title but kept working on the idea. The original project did what many do in Hollywood: it evolved.

Fast-forward in time. Roger Allers and Rob Minkoff were put in charge as co-directors. Sketches and story possibilities soon

Who has won more Academy Awards than anyone? Walt Disney!

populated their workrooms. But all these possibilities needed to coalesce into something that made sense, that told a story—an appealing story that both kids and adults would enjoy.

After six months of working on story development, it was clear that what they had was a bunch of great ideas, but what they still didn't have was a story. In business terms, they had completed the "divergent thinking" stage (coming up with new ideas) and needed to move into the "convergent thinking" stage where those ideas are synthesized. Put simply: someone needed to start making decisions.

A brainstorming meeting was held for two days in which ideas were tossed in and tossed out. Lots of "what ifs?" came and went. Characters were sketched, and characters were erased. It was a collaborative, creative process with many facets to think about.

If the story is about a son who will inherit his father's kingdom, that means the father must die. That risks making the kids cry. Great stories need a villain. Making the villain the king's brother would increase the drama. A family rivalry hinted at Shakespeare's *Hamlet*. Bringing in a girl lion would add some *Romeo and Juliet*.

A coherent, engaging story was starting to take shape. Elements of the Biblical stories of Moses and Joseph were incorporated, along with the 1942 Disney classic, *Bambi*. *Bambi* also exclusively featured talking animals, presented in a naturalistic setting, and included the death of a parent. In fact, when writer Irene Mecchi joined the team, she was told that the story pitch was "Bambi in Africa meets Hamlet." She nicknamed the project "Bamlet." The movie that Roy O. Disney (Walt's older brother) had described as being about "knowing who you are and being true to yourself" was becoming more sophisticated.

Before the writers were done, many characters and subplots came and went. Some of the characters cut from the original script were Mheetu, Nala's brother; Bhati, a bat-eared fox; and Joka, a rock python. There was also a rhino with a tickbird on his back. Actually, the tickbird evolved into Zazu, who would go on to become a very important character in both the movie and the musical.

There is a very sad scene in which Mufasa dies. According to the makers, the scene was originally even more heartbreaking, but when a test audience of children saw the preview, they started to sob uncontrollably. The scene was softened before the movie was released.

Animation Drama

With the story taking shape, it was time to send some of the lead production crew to Africa. The animators saw the big sky, the vast **savanna**, and the mix of animals in their natural environment. They also observed African art and culture, which affected the film in subtle ways.

Back at the Disney Studios in Burbank, California, a rivalry was brewing. The movie *Pocahontas* was being animated at the same time. Which movie was going to be the more successful and thus more prestigious? That's the one people wanted to work on, of course! Many of the top animators bet on *Pocahontas*. Younger, less experienced, but equally passionate folks took on the job of animating *The Lion King*. As it turned out, the older animators bet wrong. While *Pocahontas* was a $142 million hit, *The Lion King* raked in $987 million worldwide, becoming the highest-grossing, traditionally animated film of all time.

Even without the senior animators, the team was capable of taking on the job. And what a job it was! For example, there is a sequence in which thousands of wildebeests stampede down a narrow canyon (see the link in the Further Information section). Those two and a half minutes required more than two years of work by five specially trained animators and technicians. And yes, although it was done back in the early 1990s, they used a 3D computer program. The program allowed them to multiply images of wildebeests that had been drawn on separate cels. The figures still needed to be shaded by hand to look like drawn animation and given randomized paths to simulate the real, unpredictable

Simba looks up at the stars over Pride Rock and thinks of his late father, Mufasa.

Here's a brief synopsis of the story in its final form:

This movie follows the adventures of the young lion Simba, the heir to the throne of his father, Mufasa. The kingdom, Pride Lands, is an African savanna. Simba's wicked Uncle Scar plots to grab Mufasa's throne by luring father and son into a stampede of wildebeests. Simba survives, but Mufasa is killed. Simba escapes to a jungle where he enjoys a "Hakuna Matata" (no worries) lifestyle. Simba returns as an adult to take back his homeland from Scar and begin a family of his own with his girlfriend Nala, signaling the circle of life.

movement of a herd. Their work product was called CGI, or computer-generated imagery; CGI can combine hand-drawn images with computer technology.

The completed movie required the contributions of more than 600 artists, animators and technicians; 1,197 hand-painted backgrounds; 119,058 individually colored frames of film; and more than one million drawings.

Inspiring the Animators

Taking all of the animators to Africa was too expensive. Instead, animals were brought to the animators. An adult lion and a cub served as models for anatomy and musculature and allowed the animators to study exactly how their bodies moved. World-famous wildlife expert Jim Fowler brought in other animals to be sketched by the animators. Additionally, one man did a detailed study of how various animals moved; this was used as a reference.

When something is a team effort, when everybody sees what everybody else is creating, everyone pushes each other to create the best possible product. It's common for animators to use mirrors, so they can watch how their faces change with different words or feelings. The woman who drew Zazu was known for leaping around her office to get the feel of the bird in motion.

Whether on stage or in live-action movies, the casting of actors comes late in the development process. That's not the case with animated movies. Animators relish the ability to understand the character's feelings as they sketch, because it suggests how the characters should look.

The collaboration between the animator and actor is described in a conversation between Andreas Deja, supervising animator for Scar, and Jeremy Irons, who provided the voice:

> **Deja:** I started with watching male lions ... I thought it should be very smooth, elegant, a slick, soothing quality ... but Jeremy Irons' reading brought the character to life.

> **Irons:** The pictures are drawn as a result of the sounds you are making ... You can take it very wild, very broad, and give the animator some nourishment [with which] to draw.

> **Deja:** Jeremy Irons has a way of playing with the words and twisting them, and every line that Jeremy would give me was interesting.

> **Irons:** Andreas caught all of the wickedness and all of the humor that I wanted to have in him [Scar], and more.

Jeremy Irons would win the 1994 Annie Award for Best Achievement for Voice Acting. (The Annies have been acknowledging accomplishments in animation since 1972.) Some might argue that Frank Welker also deserves an Annie Award. He's the fellow who made all of the lion sounds. That's right: the movie does not include any sounds from real lions!

Enter Tim Rice

The celebrated lyricist Tim Rice was brought on very early in the process, in 1991. A Disney favorite, he was already at the studio working on *Aladdin* when he was invited to make suggestions about how songs might be incorporated into the movie. He agreed to come on board on one condition: that a suitable composer would be joining. When his first choice—the Swedish pop group ABBA—turned it down, he pitched the movie to pop icon Elton John, who agreed with enthusiasm.

Rice worked closely with the writing team, since his songs needed to work with the narrative. As the script underwent changes, he reworked his lyrics—a process that continued until the end of the production. Of course, those changes meant the animation had to be revised as well. Mouths had to move in sync with the words.

Another important contributor to the film was originally hesitant. Composer Hans Zimmer was sought because he had done two movies with African settings and was nominated for an Oscar for his score of *Rain Man*, the winner for Best Film of 1988. Zimmer wasn't thrilled with the idea of composing the musical score for a children's animated movie. He eventually signed on because of how the story resonated with his own relationships, both with his daughter and with his father, who died when Zimmer was very young. He later said this was one of the greatest experiences in his professional career. His score for *The Lion King* did more than earn him a nomination. This time, he won the Oscar for Best Original Score.

Earthquake!

Six months before the movie was due in theaters, a unique teaser trailer ran nationwide. Disney chose to simply feature a single scene: the entire opening sequence with the song

"Circle of Life." The president of Buena Vista Pictures (which distributes Disney films) said, "We were all so taken by the beauty and majesty of this piece that we felt like it was probably one of the best four minutes of film that we've seen." The public's response was overwhelmingly enthusiastic. This caused some in management to be anxious that the picture might not live up to expectations. However, the public's response energized the crew; their renewed commitment was vital since only one-third of the picture had been completed. They would need to work fast!

Then, just a few weeks later, on January 17, 1994, a magnitude 6.7 earthquake struck the San Fernando Valley, where *The Lion King* was being produced. It was felt as far away as Las Vegas, Nevada, 200 miles (322 kilometers) to the east. The famous LA freeway collapsed, gas mains burst and caught fire, and power was lost to vast sections of the city. Nobody could get to work. While some animators were camped out in the studio, others needed to carry on in people's garages. Everyone did what needed to be done, and the movie was finished in time for its release date.

Success!

This animated movie was a huge hit from the day it opened, garnering a fistful of awards and records:

- Most successful film released in 1994

- Annie Awards for Best Animated Film and for Best Achievement for Voice Acting (Jeremy Irons)

- Oscar for Best Original Score (Hans Zimmer); top-selling soundtrack (fourteen million sold)
- Oscar for Best Original Song for "Can You Feel the Love Tonight"
- Grammy Award for Best Musical Album for Children
- Golden Globe for Best Motion Picture—Musical or Comedy
- Chosen for preservation by the United States National Film Registry of the Library of Congress as being "culturally, historically, or aesthetically significant," 2016

Since then it has been called "one of Disney's most beloved animated titles," with lifetime global box-office sales of $969 million worldwide, including $423 million domestically (as of 2017). It's also the best-selling home video of all time, with over 55 million copies sold. In September 2016, Walt Disney Studios announced that it would be producing a live-action version of *The Lion King*. In November of 2017, Disney announced a release date of July 19, 2019.

Facts You May Not Know

LIONS AND BABOONS AND CHEETAHS...
An earlier version of the film was about a battle between lions and baboons. Scar was the leader of the baboons. Rafiki was a cheetah, not a baboon. Simba became a lazy, slovenly character. Does that sound like a hit to you?

INSPIRATION OR ECHOES OF THE PAST?

Many opinions have been rendered about the literary references in *The Lion King*, which include the Bible and three of Shakespeare's plays: *Hamlet, Richard II*, and *Romeo and Juliet*.

In *Hamlet*, a young prince (Hamlet) vows to revenge his father's murder by Claudius, who is Hamlet's uncle and the brother of the murdered king. Similar relationships and events are found in *The Lion King*.

However, there are differences between *The Lion King* and *Hamlet*. While Hamlet is an adult (perhaps thirty) when his father dies, Simba is still a cub.

- Simba's sadness over his father's death is replaced with happy "Hakuna Matata" years hanging out with Timon and Pumbaa. Hamlet, on the other hand, is depressed and suicidal with some potential madness thrown in—not Disney fare. It's considered a tragedy.

- Simba has moral guides (Zazu and Rafiki) to help him make good decisions. All Hamlet has is a ghost's call for revenge—not at all the same.

- At the end, Simba and Nala start a family, while Hamlet and Ophelia never get married. In fact, they both die at the end of the play.

- Most of the characters in *Hamlet* die. In *The Lion King*, only the uncle and father die.

Admittedly, there are lines taken from Shakespeare's works that were inserted to amuse parents. For example, in *Romeo and Juliet*, Juliet asks her lover, "What's in a name?" In "Hakuna Matata," Timon sings, "Oh, what's in a name?" In the play *Hamlet*, Prince Hamlet addresses the skull of the dead court jester Yorick. Similarly, in *The Lion King*, Scar holds a skull while singing along with Zazu, the red-billed hornbill.

Other sources claim that *The Lion King* derives at least in part from an epic tale still told by West African *griots* (history keepers, or storytellers, like Rafiki). In the story, the original king of ancient Mali in West Africa is Sundiata, whose name translates as "the lion king." After his father dies, Sundiata is banished from his homeland. He later returns to his kingdom and battles the evil sorcerer king who has overtaken it in his absence.

Thinking back over the process of how the screenplay was written, it seems unfair to say that the movie was *Hamlet*-inspired because it ignores the role of the original National Geographic project and the brainstorming process.

Here's how Roy Disney, then-Vice Chairman of The Walt Disney Company, viewed the derivation of *The Lion King*: "I think *The Lion King* really refers back to a lot things we've done in the past, like *Bambi*: using animal allegories to tell human stories."

What do you think—inspiration or echoes from the past?

Chapter 2

From Screen to Stage

The Walt Disney Company was not always the powerhouse that it is today. After Walt Disney died in 1966, the company struggled through the 1970s and 1980s. To fend off "corporate raiders," who wanted to buy the weakened company, the Disney family brought in Michael Eisner as chief executive officer (CEO) in 1984. Eisner had an impressive record of accomplishment at ABC as senior vice president in charge of programming and development, and then as president and chief operating officer (COO) of Paramount Pictures. He moved Paramount from last to first place among the six major movie-production studios.

The first person he hired was theatrical producer Peter Schneider, who in turn hired more theater professionals.

Opposite: Mufasa and Young Simba performed in Singapore in 2011.

As CEO, Michael Eisner took Disney to the next level.

These new hires included lyricist Howard Ashman and his long-time collaborator, composer Alan Menken, who wrote the songs for Disney's 1989 animated musical *The Little Mermaid*—the first such movie to have more of a "Broadway feel." The critical and commercial success of *Mermaid* led to Ashman and Menken teaching Disney creatives how to develop animated musicals rather than animated movies.

Then, in 1991, Walt Disney Pictures had a box-office hit with their adaptation of the fairy tale *Beauty and the Beast*. The movie set a record as the highest-grossing animated film. The *New York Times* theater critic Frank Rich must have tuned into this change of style at the Disney Studios by writing that *Beauty and the Beast* was "a better musical" than anything he'd seen on Broadway that year. Inspiring words, as it turned out.

Disney Decade

Eisner's goal was to make the '90s the "Disney Decade" that would expand existing parks, build new ones here and abroad, produce new movies, and invest in new media.

As part of that initiative, Eisner needed to find additional sources of revenue. He was aware that some Broadway musicals—like *Cats, Les Misérables,* and *The Phantom of the Opera*—were enormous hits, earning millions of dollars. The decision was made to launch Disney Theatrical Productions.

Beauty and the Beast opened on April 18, 1994 as Disney's first musical on Broadway. It was a hit with families but a miss with the critics. The show was not only considered a literal translation of the movie but lambasted as "bloated, padded, gimmick-ridden, tacky, and despite the millions [spent on the production], utterly devoid of imagination."

However, David Richards, the reviewer for the *New York Times* saw it in a larger context:

> As Broadway musicals go, *Beauty and the Beast* belongs right up there with the Empire State Building, F.A.O. Schwarz and the Circle Line boat tours. It is hardly a triumph of art, but it'll probably be a whale of a tourist attraction.

Eisner's choice of a director for *Beauty* had been someone with experience directing live shows at the Disney theme parks. To his credit, Eisner realized that in order for the musical to be a critical success, he would need people with theater experience.

Importantly, Eisner had the determination to not wait to see how the public or the critics would receive the new musical. He was going for it. His new theatrical division would need two things, both of which required time: new options for stage productions, and theaters in which to show them.

Laying the Groundwork

Let's start with the theater itself, because it shows us the depth of the commitment Disney was making to live theater. In 1992, Eisner started looking at the New Amsterdam Theatre in Times Square as a potential home. Signing that lease was noteworthy not only because the lease was so long (forty-nine years) but because the place was run down. And the neighborhood was worse. Nowadays, it's filled with tourists. But back then, tourists knew to avoid it.

Eisner also began meeting with Thomas Schumacher, who produced *The Lion King*, to identify old animated films and new nonanimated titles to consider staging. Eisner was most interested in the possibility of adapting *The Lion King* for the stage. Schumacher told Eisner repeatedly that turning *The Lion King* into a musical was the *worst* idea he'd ever heard. Not only were there no people at all in the movie, but everyone in America—practically—had seen it and knew it by heart. "I told him it was impossible." Eisner's comeback was that no, it wasn't impossible—Schumacher just needed to have "a great idea."

Schumacher later said, "I [finally] had one really great idea, and that was Julie Taymor."

Although Schumacher had been working in Los Angeles producing theater and other performance art in the 1980s, he had heard about Julie Taymor and her extraordinary production of *Liberty's Taken* on the opposite coast, in Massachusetts. He continued to hear about her as a brilliant director, innovative designer, and avant-garde conceptualist.

Times Square was once a seedy area, not the theater mecca it is today.

As he worked with her, Schumacher came to realize that what he saw as "impossible," she saw as wonderfully challenging. Rather than being worried about recreating something that theatergoers would already know so well, she was excited about the possibility of creating an experience that people would again feel in their hearts. Determined to earn a positive response from theater critics, Eisner gave the green light to hiring Taymor. She would create one of the most technically complicated and visually astonishing productions in Broadway history.

THE CREATIVE TEAM

Director: Julie Taymor

Choreographer: Garth Fagan

Music and Lyrics: Elton John and Tim Rice

Additional music and lyrics: Lebo M, Mark Mancina, Jay Rifkin, Julie Taymor, and Hans Zimmer

Book: Roger Allers and Irene Mecchi, adapted from the screenplay by Irene Mecchi, Jonathan Roberts, and Linda Woolverton

Sets: Richard Hudson

Costumes: Julie Taymor

Mask and puppet design: Julie Taymor and Michael Curry

Lighting: Donald Holder

The Big Experiment

Julie Taymor was the person most responsible for creating this innovative musical. She "reimagined" the movie. Additionally, she designed the costumes, codesigned the masks and puppets, contributed additional lyrics, and directed the production. *The Lion King* would become known for its innovations. Considering Julie Taymor's prior experience, it's easy to see how she creatively transferred her theatrical and storytelling skills to *The Lion King*.

Although Taymor turned out to be a superb choice, putting her in charge of this project required a great deal of faith. In Hollywood, she was a virtual unknown. She had never done anything commercial on the scale of a Disney project. Her reputation was as "an obscure avant-garde experimentalist." There was much joking speculation about the artistic marriage of the corporate giant and this maverick artist.

In an interview she revealed: "I want to break people's expectations, to shake them up, to shock them. That's the whole point of doing theater." Now put that next to Disney's vision: "to deliver stories, characters, and experiences that are welcomed into the hearts and home of millions of families around the world." It was a brave corporate gamble for Disney to trust Taymor to effectively merge her bold, multicultural experiences with the big-budget glitz of Broadway.

In fact, Disney referred to the entire project as "the big experiment." With the exception of lyricist Tim Rice, no one on the entire creative team, including Julie Taymor, had any Broadway experience. What's more, using masks and puppets in a Broadway show was unconventional, to say the least. Taymor had used them for years, but never in a production that aimed to be a commercial success. In the afterword of her book, *The Lion King: Pride Rock on Broadway,* Taymor expressed appreciation for the risk Disney was taking:

It is rare to have an opportunity to experiment, take risks, and develop a piece of theatrical art that is intended to be commercial as well. The merging of these two worlds is a rare phenomenon.

Conceptualizing

Schumacher, as the producer, remarked: "The biggest challenge was for the audience to accept that the people they're seeing onstage are representing animals." Taymor seems to have seen it not as a technical question but rather as a storytelling issue. She felt that although this is a story told with animals, it is a human tale. Consequently, she wanted humans revealed at all times. In the musical, the audience sees the mask but also sees the actor wearing the mask. She refers to this as a "double event."

She extended this approach further. In movies, special effects are like secret magic tricks. They often cause the audience to wonder, "How did they DO that?" Taymor took the opposite approach in *The Lion King*. She chose to reveal to the audience the *how* by showing the ropes, pulleys, and wires that create the magic. She believes that when special effects are hidden, the audience is passive. But by revealing the inner workings of its magic, *The Lion King* invites the audience to actively use their imaginations to "fill in the blanks." We'll get more into the masks, puppets and the rest, but let's follow Taymor's process.

Writing a Stronger Story

Turning a kids' Disney movie into a Broadway musical presented a number of challenges. Taymor uses the word "challenge" multiple times in her book about the show. These broad challenges would be addressed in a process called "reimagining."

Where would you begin your process of reimagining this movie? Taymor's starting point was the story's through-line of the young hero, Simba. In just eighty-eight minutes, there was not enough time for Simba to take a journey that would allow him to earn his rightful place as king. A two-act production would provide the required time. As she wrote in her book:

In every prodigal-son story the hero needs to pass certain trials, tests that hurdle him to the bottom before he is allowed to come back on top. Simba, in this coming-of-age saga, needed to earn his homecoming to Pride Rock.

For Simba to take on such trials, the show would need a character older than the little cub in the movie. Taymor reimagined his character as "a troubled and lost teenager [with] more bite and a rebellious edge." Scott Irby-Ranniar, then thirteen years old, would originate the role of Young Simba on Broadway.

Another reason why the book would need to be an expansion of the screenplay stems from the ability of pictures to quickly convey so much information. A great example of this is the scene in the movie in which Mufasa is walking with little Simba. It shows Simba's little paw stepping into the huge footprint of his father, and right away it's understood how the young lion feels: he'll have to do a whole lot of growing to be as great as his father.

The need to expand the screenplay also created opportunities. While the movie was very popular with the public, Taymor firmly believed—as some critics also had remarked—the movie lacked strong roles for women. To emphasize the women in the narrative, she made several changes.

Rafiki was not only changed into a female baboon but became "a strong, essential feminine presence" and the story's spiritual guide. To further emphasize what Taymor called "the absolute humanity of this character," the decision was made that Rafiki would be the only cast member with neither a mask nor a puppet.

The role of Simba's best friend, Nala, was also expanded importantly. In the movie, Nala leaves Pride Lands merely to forage for food. But in Act II of the stage production, Nala goes to Scar to complain that there is no food or water, only to have him come on to her. Nala rejects him and must flee Pride Lands. Going into exile brings on deep sadness and loneliness, making Nala's tale as compelling as Simba's.

Enhancing the Score

As we've seen, both the movie's score and individual songs were wildly popular. Kids especially loved singing "Hakuna Matata." So, the music was off to a great start. But while the film had just five songs, a typical musical has twelve or fifteen musical numbers. As luck would have it, a wonderful album, *Rhythm of the Pride Lands*, had been produced in 1995 as a "sequel" to the soundtrack of the film.

For this album, the composers had written new songs, mostly in Zulu, with a strong African choral center. Zulu songs? Again, Taymor didn't see that as a problem, explaining in her book:

What personality traits do you read in Nala's mask?

I was keen to keep these songs in Zulu as nothing can replace the poetry and mystery of the sound of the language, and it is totally unimportant to understand the literal meaning of words at various places in the piece.

The fact that none of the composers of this Broadway musical were Broadway theater people was very freeing for them. There was no one saying, "Oh, but that's not how we do it on Broadway." They created music that was a new fusion of African and pop. The use of African choral singing plus lots of wonderful percussion instruments like kalimbas, marimbas, and balophones provide the African soundscape.

Circle as Metaphor

Now that the story, characters, and score were conceptualized, it was time to think about the look of the show. What had been emerging as the central theme, as Taymor thought of it, was the notion of the circle of life. The use of this metaphor was extended by Taymor because she saw it embodied in the father–son relationship and the position of king; she saw it also in the cyclical weather pattern of drought and rejuvenation in the life cycle of the savanna. Working with scenic designer Richard Hudson, the circle was to become the key thematic element of the design. The circle would represent everything being right and balanced in the world, starting with the rising sun in the opening scene.

The metaphor of a circle also inspired the design of Pride Rock. As Taymor first pictured it, a spiral turntable could rise up out of the stage, like a wedding cake carousel. This would achieve two things that were important to the director. It would, from the start, let the audience know that this show was going to be a fresh take, stimulating them to release any expectations that this musical was going to be a rehash of the movie. This was especially important given the criticisms of its predecessor, *Beauty and the Beast*.

The second thing that was important to Taymor was engaging the audience as participants rather than as passive spectators. Letting them see all of the stage mechanics of Pride Rock would be one of many techniques she would employ to achieve this. Ordinarily, movies and television shows keep the technical side of things well hidden. But in theater, revealing how special effects are created, and how sets and costumes are designed, can be a very effective way of deepening audience engagement. It can allow them to use their imaginations to fill in whatever has been deliberately left out or only hinted at. Her creative methods and style of working are also evident in the way she designed the animal characters in *The Lion King*.

No Fuzzy Costumes

Roger Allers, who codirected the movie, joined forces with Taymor early in the process. Like some of his fellow team members, he was skeptical of her approach. The thought of "characters prancing around in fuzzy costumes" was really unappealing to Allers. However, his initial apprehension turned to excitement when he learned what Taymor was thinking about.

When Taymor had watched the movie, the "rich humanity" of the animal characters was one of the things she found most compelling. She observed that people were moved to laugh or cry as they not only listened to the dramatic voices but also watched the characters' expressive faces. If she were to put a mask on an actor, the actor's ever-changing face would not be seen. And then there was the practical issue of alienating great actors who don't want their faces hidden and singers who want their voices heard and not muffled by a mask. Plus, an animal costume would inhibit a performer's ability to move or dance.

Taymor began designing by focusing on the giraffe, a zebra, a herd of gazelles, and a flock of birds. That particular set of animals seems like a very challenging place to start, which might be why she chose it, since she loves nothing better than a challenge worthy of her talents. She firmly believed that she could trust the audience to fill in with their imagination.

Surprisingly, what she came up with for the giraffe was putting the actor on four stilts. OK, that makes the actor tall. Now what about that long neck? She decided that the long neck and the head of the giraffe would be worn like a tall hat on the actor's head. That way, the actor's face would be visible. She loved the notion of giving the audience an opportunity to both enjoy and appreciate seeing the dancer as part of the giraffe.

What about that herd of gazelles? Wonder how she handled that challenge? Answer: brilliantly! She used a technique she calls "corporate puppetry." One dancer could have a gazelle on her head and one gazelle on each arm. That way, five dancers would become a herd of fifteen gazelles leaping across the stage. Armed with these ideas for how to show both the actor and the animal, she felt ready to think about the main characters, starting with Mufasa, the king, and Scar, his envious brother.

Starting the Mufasa and Scar Masks

To create the puppets and masks, Taymor called on Michael Curry, with whom she had collaborated so effectively before. Taymor's expertise was the aesthetic design of the characters, and she would be actually sculpting the masks. Curry's forte was technical design of their materials and manipulation. Because of their history, they knew that each would be involved in the work of the other. Curry would weigh in about the look of the show, and Taymor would contribute to how the characters would be moving on the stage.

As with the creation of the giraffe, gazelles, and other characters, they began by generating concepts for how these masks would work. Look up the definition of mask and you'll see "a cover or partial cover for the face." So there's the conundrum: how can you make a mask that covers but does not cover a face? This is where Curry's skills in technical design would be most critical.

Their first solution was a shield mask that actors could either hold in front of them or wear on their arms or backs. The original Scar mask was actually in two halves that the actor could wear on his arms. The designers appreciated that this split-mask approach would allow them to emphasize the two sides of Scar's split personality: charming and mean. That original design morphed into a shield mask that the actor would either hold in front with both hands or slip up and over his head into a backpack. Both of these ideas were taken to the prototype stage but ultimately scrapped as unworkable for the actors.

While Curry was exploring the technical possibilities of the masks, Taymor was sculpting with clay. Because a mask has one fixed look, she needed to find an expression that captured the character's dominant trait. She uses the term ideograph to refer to a visual image that represents a concept. Mufasa is compassionate yet powerful and fearsome. She also saw him as very balanced, straightforward. Highly visual in her thinking,

Taymor translated "balanced" into "symmetrical." Mufasa would have a symmetrical face surrounded evenly with a mane, symbolizing the circle of life that was at the core of her vision.

To contrast with the symmetry of Mufasa's mask, she gave Scar's mask a twisted face with one eyebrow up and one down. While the Mufasa mask was about smoothness, Scar's was about angularity and boniness. Looking at these two masks, Taymor was pleased that the pair also captured the three things that mattered: Disney, Africa, and her own aesthetic.

Commitment

For this next phase of the production process, the team needed to grow enormously. African-born British designer Richard Hudson was brought in to develop the scenery. Taymor sought out Garth Fagan to choreograph. Designers for lighting and sound were selected. The musical score needed to be adapted by a trio of orchestrators. Other specialists were required to design wigs and makeup, and to create final sketches and begin making more than 250 costumes. Soon, a huge loft space in New York City was filled with artists of all types, working with music and maquettes, drawings and saws. Armed with lots of cups of coffee. Taking all this in, producer Thomas Schumacher underlined the boldness of this journey:

> The irony here is that the most competent, most successful entertainment company working in the world today [Disney] has set out to make its most daring, most challenging piece thus far, and it is doing it by committing to artists, not by committing to a business proposition.

Next Up: Puppets

The creative team's development of masks can be called an "iterative process." That's a business term that means, basically, "keep coming up with ideas until you discover something that works." Taymor and Curry would go through that same process when designing puppets that would transform the actors into animals. A particular challenge was creating Timon, the endearing meerkat.

Meerkats are typically only a foot tall, so turning an actor into a meerkat was going to be, well, a stretch. Taymor and Curry needed to draw on their combined experience with puppets to create something that worked for Timon. One idea they came up with was a form of Japanese puppetry in which the performer sits on a squat, wheeled "hachiochi" stool with the puppet's feet attached to his own. OK, so the actor would look smaller, but the reality of an actor scooting around on a stage created too many problems. Scrap that.

Trying another approach, they considered using a "humanette." In this technique, the actor (standing) holds a puppet in front, with his hands manipulating the puppet's arms. The puppet's feet are attached to the actor's knees, while the head comes up to the actor's chin. This allows the actor freedom of movement and leaves the actor's face visible. Sounds good so far. Oh, but wait. This meerkat seems to be hovering three feet above the stage. A floating meerkat is not in the script. Scrap that, too.

Fortunately, there were more puppet styles in Taymor's bag of tricks—a "bag" she developed by spending years in Indonesia working with puppetry and masks. It was there that she learned about the Bunraku style of puppetry. In this

DIRECTOR JULIE TAYMOR

Julie Taymor won a Tony award as the Best Director of a Musical in 1997, the first woman to do so. While *The Lion King* was her first commercial success, it was not her first show, by any means. She's known for "thinking outside of the box" not only because she has a creative imagination, but also because she has a rich and diverse background in the performing arts.

When you were a kid, did you put on shows in your backyard with your siblings or friends? Julie Taymor did. When she was just sixteen, she left home to study at L'Ecole de Mime in Paris "for some physical discipline." At Oberlin College in Ohio, she majored in folklore and mythology to get her storytelling chops and studied ensemble acting.

With a Watson Fellowship and later a Ford Foundation grant, she took herself to Indonesia to explore visually oriented theater as well as experimental and traditional puppetry. Intending to spend a few months, she instead spent several years, immersing herself in the rich storytelling traditions of the region: Bunraku puppetry, Chinese opera, Japanese butoh dance theater, hand puppetry, shadow puppets, and stick puppets.

It was while studying and working as a choreographer in Java that she experienced theater that is rehearsed and performed within the community setting. This is a complete reversal of Western theater, which relies heavily on a fourth wall, keeping the audience at a distance.

Upon returning to the United States, Taymor seized many opportunities to apply and extend her creativity. She worked in theater, opera, and film, often working with not-for-profit theaters the National Endowment for the Arts (NEA) was intended to support.

She began by designing costumes, masks, puppetry, and choreography, but by 1995, she would begin focusing on directing. During these varied productions, she developed the theatrical style for which she would be known: mixing theatrical techniques from around the world, a reverence for the art of storytelling, an ability to manipulate scale and distance to give the production a cinematic look, and a respect for the audience's imagination.

Director Julie Taymor with the asymmetrical mask she created for Scar

In an interview about *The Lion King*, Taymor declared:

> You know what I love about *The Lion King*? It's really theater operating in its original sense, which is about family and society. It's doing exactly what theater was born for— to reaffirm where we are as human beings in our environment.

classical Japanese art form, three puppeteers manipulate a puppet about four feet in height. But some adaptations were needed. For one, a single actor would manipulate the Timon puppet, using animatronics from the science of robotics. Also, rather than spending more than a half century training to become a master Bunraku artist, the American actor would get a two-week workshop. His or her skills would be honed during six weeks of rehearsals, plus a couple more weeks in previews.

Scenic Design

At this point in the process, attention was now focused on the scenic, or set, design. Richard Hudson, the designer, rejoiced in the freedom of *The Lion King*, in that it does not take place in any specific time. He felt this gave him boundless possibilities "so long as the scenery evoked Africa, and so long as it helped tell the story." While much of his experience was in designing for London opera, he had been born in Zimbabwe, in southern Africa. The seemingly endless landscape and sky of Africa were familiar to him.

The vast panorama of the African savanna, with its wide-open sky, is relatively easy to paint on a gel for the movie. It's quite something else to create this vista on a proscenium stage—which is really just a box. Hudson, along with Taymor and the lighting designer, Donald Holder, studied the physical and technical specifics of both the New Amsterdam Theatre on Broadway and The Orpheum in Minneapolis, where they would be doing the preopening run.

To extend the look of the stage, the team designed 30-foot (9.1 meters) light boxes to replace the standard wings on each side of the stage. These translucent Plexiglas columns were hung with lighting instruments, so the entire stage could be wrapped in a continuous tone of color, much like the African sky. This is just one example of how the director, scenic designer, and lighting designer collaborated to devise innovative solutions that would enhance the show.

A critical part of the scenic design would be Pride Rock. Its design, like everything else, went through a metamorphosis. Hudson felt Taymor's tiered "wedding cake" was too neat, too safe. He drew from his own experience, in this case a revolving staircase he created for an opera by the nineteenth-century Italian composer Verdi. This would create the unlikely mix of Italian opera with Japanese puppetry and a Disney animated movie.

August 1996 Workshop

It was then time to fly to Orlando, Florida, for a two-week-long workshop. Everyone knew it was really a test. Disney senior management needed to believe that this imaginative production was going to be a winner.

Some elements went over very well, starting with the reading of the script. *Check!* Models of the sets and designs of the costumes? *Check* and *check!* Puppets of the nasty hyenas and the lovable Pumbaa, the warthog? *Love 'em!* But there the enthusiasm ended. Zazu, the all-important advisor to Mufasa, simply did not work when portrayed by an actor. He was simply too big, and too awkward, to be believable as a hornbill. They needed to revisit the idea of turning Zazu into a puppet that would be held and manipulated by the actor.

Additionally, the masks for Mufasa and Scar weren't moving in tandem with the actors; they needed a technical redesign.

Of huge importance was the fact that the Disney people were still not convinced about Taymor's central concept of the animal/human "double event," which allows the audience to see the actor as well as the animal they are playing. Management declared that they wanted to see several alternatives, including the traditional approach of using makeup, as was done for the successful musical *Cats*.

Taymor, both open-minded and yet always willing to fight for what she believes in, was ready to rethink the challenge and create new prototypes—with one condition. She insisted that the next evaluation, in February of 1997, would have to be done not in another conference room but in the actual New Amsterdam Theatre, on a fully lit stage, with Disney executives sitting in the audience. They would be seeing fully finished costumes, puppets, masks, and makeup—and they would be seeing it all at a realistic distance. That was an expensive "ask," but Disney agreed.

Adding Animatronics

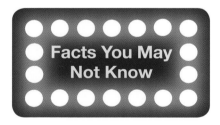

THE FACE OF SIMBA
Simba's mask took thirty-four hours to create. The mane is made of horsehair and hand-cut leather. The face is hand-painted to look like wood, but it's carbon graphite. The mask weighs less than 16 ounces (.45 kilograms), the same as a football.

Among the disadvantages of the shield concept for the Mufasa and Scar masks was the fact that when the mask was placed in the actor's backpack, there was no longer the duality of the human face plus the mask. It was "either/or." Taymor wanted "and."

With Curry's technical expertise, they devised a brand new idea, again using animatronics. The actor would wear the mask above his head. Then, using a cable hidden in his sleeve, the actor could move the mask down to cover his face. At last, the duality of actor and animal could be seen by the audience. Another important benefit was that, when the mask was lowered, the actor could assume a horizontal animal shape, using swords (Mufasa) or a cane (Scar) for support.

February 1997

After seeing several different concepts—ranging from the traditional use of makeup to Taymor's innovative double event—Eisner gave Taymor's concept his approval. His reasoning was "the bigger the risk, the bigger the reward." At last, she had the final green light. The show, as Taymor conceived of it, was bound for Broadway. Of course, if ever a show needed a few weeks out of town before opening on Broadway, it was certainly *The Lion King*. Next stop: the Orpheum Theatre in Minneapolis for a pre-Broadway run and a chance for the design team to identify and fix any unforeseen problems. And they would see plenty.

CHOREOGRAPHER GARTH FAGAN

"What am I going to do with Disney?" That was Garth Fagan's skeptical response when he learned that Disney was considering him as the choreographer for *The Lion King*. "At first, I really didn't want to do it. My kids were grown; my grandkids were grown. I hadn't seen the movie of *The Lion King*."

Two things changed his mind: falling in love with the movie, and learning that Julie Taymor and Tom Schumacher were involved. "These were people who knew what theater was about—not just [corporate types in] suits, you know," he adds, laughing. For his "path-breaking choreography," he would win the 1998 Tony Award for Best Choreography, followed by six more awards.

When he began working on *The Lion King*, Fagan had been to Africa seven times and trusted his understanding of how the animal characters should move. Quick-witted, he added: "The only problem is, they don't have to do eight shows a week, like my dancers! So I had to keep in mind that it should look like the animal, but there's a human being in there."

For Fagan, the most challenging aspect of the production was the puppets, which he knew would add weight. "But my dancers were completely fearless, and Michael Curry's wife was a dancer, so he understood." The most challenging routine is the final fight between the lioness and the hyenas, as they've been dancing for two hours. "There are very ferocious lifts and rolls and jetés. They need to tell their brain: 'No, you are not tired, leap!'"

Fagan's choreography includes many styles of dance: the torso-centered movement and energy of Afro-Caribbean dance, the speed and precision of ballet, the sense of weight of modern dance, and the rule-breaking experimentation of the post-moderns. "I wanted any child who came into the theater to see the dance that they had studied, and a dance they hadn't studied but that might be interesting to them."

Garth Fagan won the Tony Award for his "path-breaking choreography."

As of 2017, this Jamaican-born original continues to lead the Garth Fagan Dance Company, now in its forty-fifth season in Rochester, New York. Fagan, now in his late seventies, looks proudly at his work in *The Lion King*. "It's a blessing to see your life's work so beloved by so many cultures. We've been to every continent except Antarctica!"

Chapter 3

Broadway!

Anyone with experience in theater appreciates the importance of running tech rehearsals. The production team for *The Lion King* anticipated there would be snags to work through; they just didn't know which ones or how many. What would be your response during tech week when you discover:

- The elephant is too big to get through the door of the auditorium to walk down the aisle during the opening number. Oops!

- In the first scene, Mufasa and his queen, Sarabi, walk to the top of Pride Rock. It's 15 feet (4.5 m) high, has no railings, and it moves—and one of the actors is terrified of heights.

- The waterfall scene, the most complicated bit of action with fabric simulating the rushing waters, involved a series of complicated riggings that would require meticulous timing.

Opposite: Rafiki's costume and makeup contribute to her startling presence.

Julie Taymor accepted her Tony Award for *The Lion King* in 1998.

Throughout this process, the director's philosophy was: "One has to take risks and try for the best. But if your best isn't working, cut it. Fast." Some of their hard work in New York that got a quick cut in Minneapolis included Little Simba and Nala flying during "I Can't Wait to Be King," because the kids were spinning and the harnesses were pinching, and a shadow puppet of little Simba that appeared in Act I, which was hard to light and looked terrible.

After the tech rehearsals, there were three weeks of previews with an audience in the house. During the previews, the team encountered more challenges, but their spirits were buoyed by the lively appreciation of the audiences who ooh'd and aah'd and applauded spontaneously throughout the show. Both exhausted by the long workdays and energized by the audiences' responses, the team packed up and headed to Broadway.

The Reviews Are In

After opening night on Broadway, as much as a cast and crew enjoy drinking in the applause when the curtain comes down, what they're most eager for is the sweet taste of great reviews. The cast and crew of *The Lion King* were not disappointed:

Awe-inspiring! Broadway theater is alive again. Taymor's imaginative ideas seem limitless. It's a gorgeous, gasp-inducing spectacle. —*Time*

Simply said, Julie Taymor's staging of Disney's *The Lion King* is a marvel, a theatrical achievement unrivaled in its beauty, brains and ingenuity. —*Variety*

The breathtakingly staged Broadway adaptation of Disney's king of the cartoon jungle is an instant theater classic. —*Entertainment Weekly*

Time and again, Ms. Taymor seduces the audience into seeing what, in reality, isn't there. —*New York Times*

There is simply nothing else like it … One of the most memorable, moving and original theatrical extravaganzas in years, an enterprise that can only make the profit-propelled Disney organization even richer." —*New York Times*

That last quote was prophetic. The Broadway musical would play a major role in developing *The Lion King* into a global phenomenon. But first, here's how this show made history on Broadway.

The Lion King Breaks Records

Remember that quote from Michael Eisner about big risks yielding big rewards? Wow, was he ever right! *The Lion King* would go on to smash Broadway records. In September 2017, twenty years and 8,230 performances after it opened, it was still playing. Let's take in a few impressive statistics:

- 2014: First Broadway show to gross $1 billion—from its Broadway production *alone*. That news was so big it got picked up by publications all over the world.

- 2015: Set its twenty-fifth house record (for an eight-performance week) by taking in $2,587,925 for the week ending December 27, 2015.

- 2017: As this book was being written, the week's shows on Broadway were all sold out, meaning 13,568 people paid an average of $158.29; gross ticket sales were $2,219,979.

What about awards? You bet! *The Lion King*'s Broadway production has won:

- Six Tony Awards (and was nominated for another five):
    o Best Musical
    o Best Direction of a Musical (Julie Taymor, first woman to win)
    o Best Scenic Design (Richard Hudson)
    o Best Choreography (Garth Fagan)

- o Best Costume Design of a Musical
(Julie Taymor)

- o Best Lighting Design of a Musical
(Donald Holder)

- • Eight Drama Desk Awards (and nominated for another four), including the above plus:

  - o Outstanding Puppet Design
  (Julie Taymor and Michael Curry)

  - o Outstanding Sound Design (Tony Meola)

  - o Outstanding Featured Actress in a Musical
  (Tsidii Le Loka)

Perhaps even more than the awards and the box-office grosses, this assessment by a reporter writing for the *Guardian* in 1999 demonstrates that *The Lion King* became more than just another Broadway hit:

> You can't hide from *The Lion King* ... In New York, people put their newborn infants down for tickets to *The Lion King* as if reserving places at a swanky prep school. It's less a show than a life-changing rite of passage.

Imagine This

To see why this show became a megahit, it is necessary to do nothing more than to watch the opening of the show—now available in a 360-degree video on YouTube.

The experience would be even greater if you were seeing it live. Imagine yourself at the theater:

You're seated—possibly humming one of the songs from the show, while waiting. The curtain rises, followed by the lifting of translucent fabric to suggest clouds and mist lifting over the African savanna. You notice the raked stage is covered with stylized claw marks, then look up as a giant, shimmering, saffron sun rises. (You smile, as a friend told you that this effect is achieved with the use of thirty ribs of aluminum on which flutter silk strips.) Silence.

Suddenly, Rafiki splits the stillness by chanting "Circle of Life." The oohs and aahs from the audience begin. In response to Rafiki's call, animals begin to appear. Two gigantic, golden giraffes on stilts amble onto the stage. Soon, heads swivel and fingers point as a chorus of animal-actors appears all over the auditorium and proceeds down the aisles to the stage.

For the audience, the opening of the show becomes a series of wow moments, building until Pride Rock spirals up out of the stage with Mufasa and Sarabi at the very top. Wow, indeed! Taymor wasted no time in letting the audience know that they would be in for a brand-new experience. She wrote:

The [close] proximity of the chorus to the audience immediately reveals the duality of human and animal. Viewers are quickly transported from the two-dimensional world of film to a live, theatrical, wholly visceral experience.

Why Such a Hit?

From watching video clips or from reading what the experience of the audience is, you probably have some good guesses as to why this show has been such a megahit. Compare your ideas to these theories that reviewers and entertainment analysts have advanced to explain this record-busting phenomenon:

- "I've never seen anything like it!" has long been a common response to the show. People love new things. New cell phones, new apps, new clothing styles. And this musical surely was new. Not like *Beauty and the Beast*, which was a literal translation from film to the stage. The "you gotta see it to believe it" quality made for great word-of-mouth advertising. Marketers love word-of-mouth, since it is not only very persuasive but it's also free.

- The show invites the audience to participate. You could say it *includes* the audience from the very beginning, when the animal-actors emerge all around them, moving down the aisles to the stage, singing the opening song. Throughout the show, the audience becomes engaged in "filling in the blanks," as Taymor intended, by imagining whatever has been left out of the staging or only suggested.

- It's a multisensory experience created by the broad swaths of color, the leaping dancers, the throbbing drums. Someone posted on Facebook, "I literally cry

"CIRCLE OF LIFE" HAS THEM IN TEARS

The songs from the movie were already hits before the musical ever opened. Perhaps this is not surprising given the pairing of lyricist Tim Rice with singer-composer Elton John, one of the world's best-selling musicians. In fact, of the five Academy Award nominations for "Best Original Song" in 1994, three came from *The Lion King*. The Oscar went to their song, "Can You Feel the Love Tonight." Also nominated were "Hakuna Matata" and "Circle of Life." "Circle of Life" was nominated for a Golden Globe but again lost to "Can You Feel the Love Tonight."

While "Circle of Life" was nudged out of some top awards, its role in the musical and the movie cannot be overstated. It is played in the prologue as animals gather around Pride Rock to see the presentation of Simba. A reprise of the song is heard at the end as animals again gather around Pride Rock, this time to celebrate Simba and Nala's cub.

In an interview, Rice said he was amazed at the speed with which John composed: "I gave him the lyrics [to "Circle of Life"] at the beginning of the session at about two in the afternoon. By half-past-three, he'd finished writing and recording a stunning demo."

The potential impact of the song was recognized back in 1993 when selecting the trailer six months before the release of the movie. The

Elton John and Tim Rice enjoyed collaborating for both the movie and the musical.

theatrical teaser began with red text on a black background: "Next summer, Walt Disney Pictures will present its newest animated feature." What followed was the opening song that begins the story. The song—the entire opening sequence— was followed provocatively by "To be continued, June 1994." Audience reaction was so enthusiastic that there were concerns that the movie would not live up to expectations created by this enchanting song. They needn't have worried.

every time I see it—it is so overwhelming to my senses." Tshidi Manye, who played Rafiki in the American touring company, shared her perspective from the stage: "When that curtain goes up, you see these adults like little kids. You see them pointing and crying."

- The dancing and the music were both created to blend different styles. The music combines African and pop. The dancers are doing everything from Afro-Caribbean movements to street dancing. The resulting fusion was new and is very engaging.

- The show is part of the Disney entertainment behemoth. Disney was able to create other *Lion King* products (movies, TV programming, music, theme park attractions, merchandise, apps), so that seeing *The Lion King* on Broadway has become a "must" for many families, whether from the United States or abroad.

- Disney is a global brand. In the 2015–2016 season, eighteen percent of Broadway ticket holders came from other countries. Given the company's worldwide reach, those folks were more than likely to have been familiar with Disney products. *Forbes* magazine ranks Disney as the seventh–most valuable brand in the world, ahead of McDonalds and Nike, and number one in the leisure industry. There are productions in major cities around the world, creating greater awareness. The show's location (it moved from the New Amsterdam in 2006) at the Minskoff Theatre in the heart of Times Square ensures that tourists can't miss seeing the big, bold, black-and-yellow signage.

- It builds on the popularity of the hugely successful animated film. Many in the audience come in ready to sing along with "Hakuna Matata."

- Some would say that the show's popularity can also be attributed to the story, which is familiar, positive, and has global appeal.

- Business people add that savvy marketing, including dynamic pricing, is also a factor in the show's continued success.

While not often theorized as explaining its appeal, there's a level of artistry and an attention to detail that the audiences may be responding to, perhaps even without their conscious awareness:

- For starters, the production has visual cohesion. Everywhere you look, you see circles: the sun, the lake, Mufasa's mane, the antelope wheel.

- Rather than plain ground, the entire expanse of the stage is scarred with huge, stylized claw marks.

- Zazu's feathers are cut from parachute silk and hand-painted. The lionesses' corsets are made by hand, using thirty thousand beads for each corset.

- All of the costumes start out as white cloth that is then dyed and hand-painted, screen-printed, or digitally printed.

One more likely reason for the show's success is the fact that it gives everyone in the audience—probably for the first time and possibly the only time—an opportunity to experience the grandeur of Africa: the beauty of the vast open land, the grace and power of its animals, and the mesmerizing quality of its music.

Dynamic Pricing Plays a Role

In addition to the show's emotional appeal and its artistic merits, there are also economic factors to consider when trying to understand its popularity. Broadway is known for, among other things, sky-high prices for the best seats. For the smash hit *Hamilton,* the top box-office price—which is lower than resellers charge—was $849. Yes, for one seat. In June 2017, resellers were charging $1,450 for tickets to see *Hello, Dolly.* Disney made a decision that it would *not* charge exorbitant prices for the best seats, as they wanted to make the show accessible to families. Mom, Dad, and the kids can see the show without spending more than their monthly mortgage payment. The most expensive seats go for around $200.

In order to hold down their top price and yet maximize their revenues, Disney has utilized a technique called "dynamic pricing." Dynamic pricing is a method of setting and adjusting prices to reflect demand. For example, when more people want to see a particular football game or fly during a popular season, the prices go up. When there is less demand, the prices go down to attract customers. Theaters were "late to the game" of using dynamic pricing in setting ticket prices. Disney was the first to use it, and they are now considered the best at it.

Its process involves two steps. First, it forecasts what the demand will be for any given day based on historical data for box-office receipts. That gives Disney the information it needs to set prices for the different sections of the theater for the coming season. Then, once the tickets go on sale, demand is monitored for each performance. This data is used to adjust the prices up or down to increase revenues.

Marketing Smarts

While the large creative team was working on the production, a smaller but equally creative team was working on the marketing of the Broadway show. After all, seats need to be filled. Disney knew that it was going to take years of sold-out performances for the company to make back its investment before it could begin to realize a profit. (It took four years.)

To promote the musical, Thomas Schumacher, then president of Disney Theatrical Productions, turned to Nancy Coyne, known as Broadway's "marketing guru." She was the force behind *Les Misérables* and *The Phantom of the Opera*, which had prompted his interest in Broadway from the start. The strategic marketing plan ran as a test in Minneapolis the summer before the show's Broadway debut. Critics from the mainstream media were invited to preview the show, given behind-the-scenes access, and encouraged "to cover the show however they wished."

It was thought, and rightly so, that this approach would pique interest, because people were curious to see how Disney would engineer the animal-based story on stage with puppets. In New York, publicity included taxi-top ads everywhere, in

PUPPETS, MASKS, AND COSTUMES

The creative and technical process of designing the masks and puppets was a major challenge. Here are some of the little-known stories about them, now that the hard work has been addressed.

- It may seem like the actor playing Zazu might have an easier job because he is not *wearing* a puppet. Actually, it takes six weeks of rehearsal for a new actor to feel prepared, which is two weeks more than the other performers. The actor makes the wings flutter with a paddle he pulls down on the handgrip. His pointer finger controls the mouth/beak. A thumb trigger makes the eyes look neutral, surprised, or asleep.

- Simba is portrayed not only by two actors (a boy and an adult) but also by hand, rod, and shadow puppets.

- The auditioning process includes working with the puppets. According to Taymor, "The challenge is that the dancers and actors have to be game and enthusiastic to embrace that they're going to have these other appendages ... We look ... to see if they have joy or if they are going to be overwhelmed."

- The masks are made out of carbon graphite, which is what Formula 1 car frames and flooring are made of. It has a really high strength-to-weight ratio.

Here are some impressive numbers:

- 37,000 hours to build the puppets and masks

- 750 pounds (340 kg) of silicone rubber to make the masks

- 232 puppets in the show, including rod, shadow, and full-sized

- 40 hours a week spent repainting the puppets

- 27 kite birds in the show

- 25 species of animals, birds, fish, and insects represented in the show

- 18 feet (5.5 m) in height, the tallest animals in the show (giraffes)

- 13 feet (4 m) in length, the elephant from trunk to tail

- 5 inches (12.7 centimeters), the tiniest animal puppet (the trick mouse at the end of Scar's cane)

Scar's costume, weighing in at 28 pounds (12.7 kg), restricts the actor's movement. Plus, he has to deal with the electronic controllers that are housed in a large cage on his back. It requires fifteen minutes and two assistants to get him into the costume and make sure all the mechanics are working. (You can watch how an actor prepares for the role of Scar in the London production via Disney's *The Lion King* Classroom Education Series on YouTube.)

the exact colors of the show's promotional logo. It didn't hurt when talk show hostess Rosie O'Donnell, on the day after the opening, plugged the performance on her popular show.

Despite the fact that Disney's *The Lion King* has become a global phenomenon, marketing of the show continues. In an NBC interview in 2005, Coyne said, "They spend consistently, not just in weak periods. In the tourist season, you'll see a lot more outdoor [advertising], and in the winter you'll see more [ads on] television." They also have held special promotions to maintain awareness and interest. For example, they once set up a free exhibit in New York's Bryant Park, where visitors could see some of the show's design elements up close. Close to eighty thousand people attended.

With Disney Theatricals as her client, Coyne introduced "Kids Night Out," providing free admission to children accompanied by a ticket-buying adult. This has been offered during the lower-demand months of January and February. Thinking ahead with her usual acumen, she observed: "That's where the new audience comes from." She also initiated "Tuesdays at 7" which raises the curtain a full hour earlier. Why do you think she picked Tuesdays? You're right if you guessed that's the night with the smallest audiences at Broadway shows.

The Lion King pioneered the first autism-friendly Broadway performances in 2011 in conjunction with the "Autism Theatre Initiative." For these performances, the show is modified to provide an experience with quieter music, less intense lighting, and somewhat brighter house lights. "Calming areas" and relaxed rules for audience members are in effect since they are more likely to move around and make noise or sing along. Now people on the autism spectrum, and their families, are able to enjoy visiting the theater without being concerned that their sensory issues and anxiety in unfamiliar surroundings would spoil the experience for themselves or other theatergoers.

It Takes a Village

It takes a whole lot more than positive reviews and savvy marketing to keep a Broadway show up and running in tip-top form. It takes a village.

There are around fifty performers in *The Lion King* cast. Some of them perform two and even three different roles. For example, four child actresses operate the baby elephant and also alternate in the role of Nala, a young lioness. And, in an ironic twist, every ensemble member wears a grassland headpiece at some point during the show and also performs as one of the hyenas. These predators and the savanna grassland are two of the show's powerful symbols of birth and death.

Another one hundred people are involved in the daily production of the show. Among them:

- twenty-four musicians
- nineteen wardrobe staff
- thirteen carpenters
- ten electricians
- four props experts
- three makeup artists

- two hairdressers
- a child guardian
- a full-time physical therapist.

How do these people spend their time each week? Well, in wardrobe, it takes about 150 hours to keep the costumes in performance-ready condition. Those in charge of the puppets spend about forty hours a week repainting them, plus another eighteen hours checking the mechanical units and replacing the cables and batteries that make the masks and moving parts seem human.

Keep On Keeping On

Even though some members of the cast have been with the show from the start, eight hours of rehearsals are held every week. Dance supervisor Thea Barnes, who has been with the show since it opened, takes the cast through a two-hour dance class once a week to keep their moves "opening night perfect." Garth Fagan's choreography is challenging, as it combines so many styles of dance—everything from ballet to breakdancing. In addition, the stage is raked, which adds another type of strain to the performers' bodies.

The puppets themselves make different physical demands on performers. The giraffes require upper body strength, whereas other animal puppets require more suppleness and cardiovascular fitness. The whole cast has to be incredibly fit, both to provide a great show and to protect their bodies from potential injuries. This also explains why there is a physical therapist backstage at every show.

MATCHING SHOES

Each cast member's shoes are hand-painted to match their exact skin tone, with a separate jar of paint for each actor. If someone comes back from vacation with a suntan, his or her shoes are repainted to match the new skin tone.

Need for Sacrifice

In an interesting book, *Making It on Broadway*, one of the Broadway cast members writes candidly about his regrets at spending a year as Ed, the hyena that only laughs. Initially ecstatic about "catching the brass ring," he soon felt constrained. He tells of being directed to perform in a very specific way and told "don't change anything." He felt it was unfair to ask an actor to "not be creative" and to "forgo your own integrity as an artist." One can appreciate that others in the cast may also feel challenged by the demands of this show, but are willing to do it as a gift they can offer the rest of us who can't leap or sing as they do.

Jelani Remy, who joined the Broadway cast as the adult Simba in 2015, enjoys the community spirit of the cast. "Some people have been doing it since it started, so twenty years! A great mix of young and old. We have cookouts, go to the beach and generally have a great time together, because then that translates to the stage."

4

The King Rules

After opening night on Broadway, Greg Evans's review for *Variety* predicted the importance of *The Lion King* for Disney:

Simply said, Julie Taymor's staging of Disney's *The Lion King* is a marvel, a theatrical achievement unrivaled in its beauty, brains and ingenuity. Leaping far beyond its celluloid inspiration, the stage version improves upon nearly every aspect of the hit 1994 animated film ... With this production, the Walt Disney Company stages itself as a serious and ambitious contender on the legit scene, all but demanding that its first theatrical foray, 1994's too literally adapted *Beauty and the Beast* was little more than a warm-up.

Opposite: The Lion King float entertains at Disneyland Paris in 2015.

A Multimedia Franchise

The Lion King musical has been promoted and delivered to a seemingly never-ending audience. In combination with the original movie and the many spin-offs, a new entity was born: "a Disney multimedia franchise." That label means that Disney has taken an original work—in this case the animated film—and produced derivative works such as a film, a television program, or a video game. Not surprisingly, Disney has created all three, and more. It's hard to talk about the impact of the musical by itself, since it became an integral part of a collection of entertainment products.

From that first movie—which you'll remember was a risk because it was the first story the company made that was original—Disney went on to generate the following:

- Recordings (50-plus), including *The Lion King Original Cast Recording* (1997), a platinum seller

- Animated movies, including *The Lion King II: Simba's Pride* (1998), a direct-to-video sequel; *The Lion King 1½* (2004), a clever retelling of the story from the perspectives of Simba's pals, Timon (the meerkat) and Pumbaa (the warthog); *The Lion King 3: Hakuna Matata*

- A TV movie, *The Lion Guard: Return of the Roar* (2015)

- Theme park attractions (4), including *Festival of the Lion King* at Walt Disney World and Hong Kong Disneyland

- Books, such as *The Lion King*, *The Lion King II*, and *The Lion King: Six New Adventures*

- Animated TV series (2), *The Lion King's Timon & Pumbaa* (1995–1999) and *The Lion Guard* (2016–present)

- Short films (4), including *Circle of Life: An Environmental Fable* (1995)

- Video games (11)

- Currently in production is a live-action version of *The Lion King* (release: 2019).

Disney has also created two versions of the musical for schools to produce: *Disney's The Lion King Jr.* is a 60-minute version, while *Disney's The Lion King Kids* is a 30-minute version for elementary school.

Now in its third decade, *The Lion King* franchise skillfully blends the different formats in which to experience the story. For example, going to DisneyOnBroadway.com and clicking on "videos" will take you not only to "5 Fast Facts—Simba's Mask" but also an interview with Ernie Sabella, who provided the voice for Pumbaa in the movie. When the 3D version of the movie had an opening weekend of $30 million in 2011, new sales to the stage show were stimulated.

A 360-degree Experience

In 2015, Disney made available the opening number, "Circle of Life," as a 360-degree video experience. According to Disney Theatrical Productions, this "immersive video" marks the first-ever virtual reality (VR) recording of a number from a live show on Broadway. Craig Gilbert, who directed and

Using virtual reality (VR) headsets, viewers enjoy watching in 3D.

produced the video, called it a "one-of-a-kind piece." He predicted: "This could be what live theater in virtual reality can be, going forward." Other experts of digital storytelling saw this as an important evolutionary step for VR, but just a baby step.

Along with the various media, there is a plethora—a large or excessive amount—of merchandise that is offered to satisfy every yearning. Amazon lists more than 81,000 items related to *The Lion King,* with more than 1,500 on eBay. Here's a small sampling:

- Removable PVC bedroom wall stickers that say "Hakuna Matata"

BOX-OFFICE GROSS

The Top Ten Musicals ranked by box office gross as of June 2017. Shows marked with an asterisk were still running as of that date.

RANK	SHOW	$ MILLIONS
1	*The Lion King* *	$1,370
2	*Wicked* *	$1,110
3	*The Phantom of the Opera* *	$1,100
4	*Mamma Mia!*	$624
5	*Chicago* *	$586
6	*Jersey Boys*	$558
7	*The Book of Mormon* *	$493
8	*Beauty and the Beast*	$492
9	*Cats*	$408
10	*Les Misérables*	$406

Source: TheWrap.com

- *The Lion King* cupcake cake
  (how-to video with recipe)
- Easy violin sheet music
- Lion Guard power wristbands and necklaces
- Disney Baby *The Lion King* Premiere
  Convert Me Swing 2-Seat

At the time of this writing, a book on the art of *The Lion King,* signed by artists and production staff, was on eBay for $875. Nineteen people were watching this item.

Touring America

The North American touring production of *The Lion King,* begun in April of 2002, has been seen by more than nineteen million theatergoers in more than seventy cities. These productions not only contribute to the Disney balance sheet but also have an important impact on the cities they visit. The Touring Broadway League reports that, on average, Broadway tours contribute an economic impact 3.52 times the gross ticket sales to the local metropolitan area's economy. For example, a 2017 engagement of *The Lion King* in Greenville, SC, generated an estimated economic benefit of more than $19 million to the city from travel, hotels, restaurants, parking, and other businesses patronized by both theatergoers and production staff.

For the tour version, certain scenic elements have been converted. For example, not every theater would be capable of swiveling Pride Rock from beneath its stage. Most stages would not have the traps and troughs used for the entrance of the grasslands dancers and for the stampeding wildebeest scene. Starting in October 2017, the North American tour has been additionally modified to allow the musical to play in venues that previously couldn't accommodate the show.

One thing that does not change as the show tours the states is the "wardrobe bunker," with its dedicated wardrobe supervisor who oversees the organization, cleaning, and maintenance of 250 costumes, plus 100 more for the swings. It takes sixteen dressers to assist up to twelve costume changes per performer. Two days a week, a team of eight stitchers, beaders, pressers, and crafters makes repairs to keep the costumes perfect.

While Scar's wardrobe is valued at a whopping $25,000, the simplest costume is worth an impressive $500. Their value is also seen in historical terms: costumes from *The Lion King* have been added to the treasures at the Smithsonian National Museum of American History as well as the Victoria and Albert Museum in London.

Roaming the Globe

Now in its twenty-first year, *The Lion King* remains one of the most popular stage musicals in the world. It has played on every continent except Antarctica; in nineteen countries, in more than 100 cities; and to more than ninety million people (more than the combined populations of California, Texas, and New York).

Since its premiere on November 13, 1997, there have been twenty-four global productions, meaning twenty-four casts of performers, twenty-four x 232 (5,568) puppets, twenty-four Pride Rocks, twenty-four elephant graveyards, and so on. It has been performed in eight languages: Japanese, German, Korean, French, Dutch, Spanish, Mandarin, and Portuguese. Most international productions have released cast recordings. It has also meant quality control: twenty-two specialists oversee all the global productions. Director Julie Taymor stops in to spot-check each production at various stages of rehearsals or performances.

It's the only show in history to generate six productions worldwide running fifteen or more years. Ten productions are now running concurrently across the globe: in London, England's West End; Hamburg, Tokyo and Sapporo in Japan; Mexico City, Mexico; Madrid, Spain; Shanghai, China; and Scheveningen in the Netherlands, plus the American touring company and on Broadway. As an example of its global appeal, the Tokyo production, which began in 1998, achieved its ten-thousandth performance on July 15, 2015.

This overview of the musical's universal popularity helps us understand how it is that the box-office gross exceeds that of any Broadway show, of any film, or other entertainment title in box-office history. The rewards have been artistic as well as financial: it has earned more than seventy major arts awards around the world.

Lion Roars in Mandarin

The Shanghai Disney Resort opened *The Lion King* at its new Walt Disney Grand Theater in June of 2016. In

Visitors to the Shanghai Disney Resort enjoy showing what big fans they are.

the show for China, as with the shows for other cultures, elements were added to enhance the show to make it more relevant to the local culture, while maintaining the spirit of the original. It includes different regional dialects as well as riffs on Chinese pop songs. For the first time, a new character was added: the Monkey Master, based on the Monkey King—a figure of Chinese legend.

Taymor explained in an interview before the premiere that the Monkey King is China's favorite character. "These little touches of familiarity are absolutely what you have to do. It makes the show recognizable." For this character, Taymor designed a red and yellow, Chinese-inspired costume. While Monkey Master doesn't speak, he bursts in to help fight for Simba in several action scenes. The actors playing Timon and Pumbaa will not be entertaining with the Brooklyn accents used in the Broadway production; instead, they will be speaking Mandarin but with a distinct *beifang,* or northern Chinese twang, to provide a comparable slang or "attitude."

As an interesting aside, casting in China took about two and a half years, more than three times the average for this show. For starters, Broadway-style musical theater is relatively new in China. Also, Chinese actors are typically affiliated with theater companies and schools, with limited availability to work with others. In addition, Disney is thought of as an entertainment company, so there was a need to convince theater professionals that the show was an important work of genuine artistry.

Disney has recently announced that a new international tour will run from 2018 to 2020, returning to Singapore, South Korea, Taiwan, and South Africa, and adding Manila. While all productions must include some South Africans in their cast, the previous South African production used exclusively South African actors and dancers.

The Lion King Makes Broadway Golden Again

One of the biggest impacts of *The Lion King* has been on Times Square itself. Today, we think of Times Square as the mecca for theatrical productions. But it was not always so. Broadway's history is as dramatic as the productions on its stages.

Broadway's "Golden Age," from 1900 to 1930, was ended by a double-whammy: the collapse of the stock market in 1929 and the triumph of the "talkies" (films with sound) over silent films, making compelling entertainment

Times Square is now visited by over eighteen million people each year.

more available and affordable. The decline of the Times Square neighborhood continued unabated for decades. In the 1970s and 1980s, Times Square was denounced as "the most decadent city block in the western world."

In the early 1990s, word went around that Disney was thinking about getting into the business of producing musicals in New York City. Hearing of this, reporters and critics thought the notion of "Mickey Mouse on 42nd Street" was hilarious. However, Michael Eisner, CEO of The Walt Disney Company, chose to make a commitment to Times Square. For Eisner, it was a huge risk: What would it mean for a brand name of such wholesome family values to set up shop where no mom would ever think of bringing her kids? A whole lot would need to change. It's another example of Eisner taking a gamble because he believed that "big risks yield big rewards." Which is true—if they work. This one did.

Disney proceeded with a careful four-year renovation of the New Amsterdam Theatre, once the home of the Ziegfeld Follies (a series of musical extravaganzas) but long since fallen into disrepair. It was in such bad shape there were mushrooms growing on the floor. As if toppling dusty dominoes, the other theaters and retail spaces were razed or renovated as investors realized that something important was happening in Times Square.

In the 2016–2017 season, 13.3 million people attended Broadway shows, resulting in a gross of $1.45 billion. Broadway attendance topped those of the ten major league New York and New Jersey baseball, basketball, football,

and hockey teams combined (Mets and Yankees in Major League Baseball; Rangers, Islanders, and Devils in the National Hockey League; the Knicks, Liberty, and Nets in basketball, and the Giants and the Jets of the National Football League). It's no exaggeration to say that Broadway is enjoying its second Golden Age.

Disney on Broadway

When Disney's musical *Aida* opened on Broadway in March 2000, it created a trio with *Beauty and the Beast* and *The Lion King*. Perceiving an opportunity, Nancy Coyne came up with the idea of advertising the trio of Disney musicals under the collective name Disney on Broadway. This marketing technique, called "cross-selling," allowed the newer or less popular titles to ride on the coattails of the more popular and established ones. It also strengthened the Disney name as a producer of successful Broadway musicals. This strategy isn't new, as many popular products and services use this, but Coyne was the first to bring the concept to Broadway, traditionally a late starter in new marketing concepts. Currently, the Disney on Broadway trio includes *The Lion King, Aladdin,* and *Frozen.*

What's Next?

If you're wondering whether the performers of *The Lion King* went on to become celebrities, the answer is no. While that may sound disappointing, for many actors and dancers, just being able to raise a family with the earnings from their craft may be reward enough. On the other hand, there are a good many Hollywood stars who got their start doing Broadway musicals, including Sarah Jessica Parker, Nick Jonas, John Travolta, Meryl Streep, Hugh Jackman, and Kristin Chenoweth. None of them had their presence on the Broadway stage hidden by layers of face paint, masks, or puppets.

Julie Taymor, the director, continued her journey of creating interesting work in several genres. For example, she adapted, produced, and directed the movie *Titus* (1999), based on Shakespeare's play, starring Anthony Hopkins and Jessica Lange. In 2002, she earned six Oscar nominations for her movie *Frida,* the story of Mexican artist Frida Kahlo. Other movies followed, as well as operas both here and abroad. Her continuing successes are sometimes overshadowed by her highly visible dismissal in 2011 as director of Broadway's most expensive musical, *Spider-Man: Turn Off the Dark,* after nine years of work and 180 preview performances—a record. "Artistic differences" was cited as the cause.

Other members of *The Lion King* creative team, such as Richard Hudson (scenic design), Garth Fagan (dance), and those responsible for the music—Hans Zimmer, Tim Rice, and Elton John—already had terrific careers before contributing to this show. That said, their roles in bringing it to life undoubtedly added to their reputations.

Part of the Financial Picture

After reading about the success of *The Lion King*, it would be natural to think the play must be the sun around which The Disney Company must orbit. For a reality check, look at what Disney's latest annual report stated:

- Company revenues for 2016 came to $55.6 billion. Billions of dollars. Wow!

- Only 16 percent of that came from Studio Entertainment, which includes not only live stage plays (like *The Lion King*) but also live-action and animated motion pictures, direct-to-video content, and musical recordings. Studio Entertainment is one of four business segments; the others include Media Networks, Parks and Resorts, and Consumer Products & Interactive Media.

Therefore, while *The Lion King* has become a huge global franchise, it is just one element of a global entertainment giant. However, for those of us who love the musical and appreciate its journey, it remains bigger than life.

Glossary

AESTHETIC The underlying principles that guide the work of an artist. In this case, the artist is director Julie Taymor.

ANIMATRONICS In theater, film, or other entertainment, the techniques for making puppets and other objects move in lifelike fashion.

BALOPHONE A kind of wooden xylophone that plays tones when struck with a mallet, making it both percussive and melodic.

BOOK In musical theater, the book is the narrative for a musical. The book writer creates not only the dialogue but also decides where the songs will go and what they will be about.

BUSINESS PROPOSITION A business proposal or plan. In this use, the speaker is contrasting a money-making goal with an art-making goal.

CELS Shorthand for celluloid, these are transparent sheets on which scenes are drawn or painted. Cels for *The Lion King* are listed for over $2,000 each on eBay.

CONCEPTUALIST Someone who creates or grasps new ideas fully.

DERIVATIVE Products, services, or works of art that are based on another source. In *The Lion King* franchise, there are many derivative products from the original movie.

DEVELOPMENT In the process of creating a new musical, development occurs after the show is conceptualized and before rehearsals begin.

FOURTH WALL The imaginary boundary that separates the action on stage from the audience.

GROSS The total amount of revenue before expenses are factored in; the box-office gross is simply the sum of all tickets sold.

IDEOGRAPH An image or symbol that represents an idea or thing. A smiley face emoji is an ideograph for happy.

KALIMBAS African "thumb pianos," which have been around for hundreds of years.

MAQUETTE A small, preliminary model of a sculpture or a building; in this context, a model of the characters.

METAPHOR Something that is used to suggest or symbolize something else. In *The Lion King*, the circle serves as a metaphor for balance, harmony, and continuity.

MUSICAL SCORE Also known as a film score or movie soundtrack, this is the original music written for a film.

ORCHESTRATORS People who compose or arrange music.

PROSCENIUM STAGE The most common type of stage; it is shaped like a box in front of the audience and is framed by a square or an arch through which the audience views the action. Uncommon stages have an apron allowing the audience to sit on three sides of the stage.

PROTOTYPE An early sample of something.

RAKED STAGE One that is angled so that the back, which is furthest from the audience, is higher. This allows the audience to more easily see performers in the back, or "upstage."

REPRISE In music, the repetition of opening material. You can hear the reprise of "Circle of Life" here: https://www.youtube.com/watch?v=iRdeNPVoy88.

SAVANNA A wide open plain with coarse grasses and scattered tree growth. The African savannas cover almost 65 percent of the continent.

SCREENPLAY The script of a movie, which includes the lines to be spoken along with acting instructions and directions such as "cut to" or "dissolve to."

SWINGS Performers in musical theater who understudy several chorus and/or dancing roles. If an understudy fills in for a lead, a swing will act the parts normally performed by the understudy.

SYMMETRICAL Balanced, having sides or halves that are the same. Typically seen as beautiful, harmonious.

VISUAL COHESION An appealingly consistent look.

BOOKS

Bjorklund, Ruth. *Costume Design in Theater.* Exploring Theater. New York: Cavendish Square Publishing, 2017.

Capaccio, George. *Lighting and Sound in Theater.* Exploring Theater. New York: Cavendish Square Publishing, 2017.

Capaccio, George. *Puppetry in Theater.* Exploring Theater. New York: Cavendish Square Publishing, 2017.

Finch, Christopher. *The Art of The Lion King.* New York: Hyperion, 1994.

Taymor, Julie. *The Lion King: Pride Rock on Broadway.* New York: Hyperion, 1997.

WEBSITES

Disney The Lion King Experience
http://www.lionkingexperience.com

This program is described as "an immersive, project-based exploration of theater-making." There is a Junior Edition so middle-school students can produce a 60-minute version of the show, and a 30-minute Kids Edition for elementary-school students.

Broadway: The American Musical Online
http://www.pbs.org/wnet/broadway/shows/the-lion-king

Learn about *The Lion King*, then check out the Timeline for a bigger perspective on the history of Broadway.

Garth Fagan Dance
https://www.garthfagandance.org

Enjoy seeing his dancers captured in motion. Then search for "Garth Fagan Dance" on YouTube to see them in action.

VIDEOS
Behind the Scenes in *The Lion King's* Puppet Shop
https://www.youtube.com/watch?v=rvCgPRzOa3s

Go backstage to visit the musical's puppet shop, where puppet supervisor Michael Reilly shows the numerous intricate and varied puppets and masks used in the performance and walks through how they're maintained in his traveling workshop.

"Circle of Life" Spontaneously Sung on Plane
https://ohmy.disney.com/music/2014/04/01/you-have-to-see-this-video-of-the-cast-of-the-lion-king

Enjoy this impromptu performance on a flight from Brisbane to Sydney. The cast had just had an amazing day at *The Lion King* Brisbane season launch.

Disney's *The Lion King* Classroom Education Series

https://www.youtube.com/watch?v=GJkUKcNcfR0

A terrific ten-part series that uses video to provide great information about every aspect of this production. Part 4, "An Actor Prepares," goes behind the scenes with Scar.

ESPN Delves into Puppets

https://www.facebook.com/TheLionKingUSA/videos/10155248134157580/

A performer as a cheetah and the actor working with Zazu are examined with a scientific eye by ESPN Sport Science.

ESPN Visits *The Lion King*

https://www.facebook.com/TheLionKingUSA/videos/10155140384387580/

Join ESPN Sport Science as it goes backstage to examine the quickness, balance, and power of three cast members of *The Lion King* on Broadway.

The Lion King - Hakuna Matata (Musical Multilanguage)

https://www.youtube.com/watch?v=8nRhY3ISADQ

Enjoy this favorite song in French, Japanese, Spanish, German, Dutch, and English.

The Lion King: From Cub to King

https://www.youtube.com/watch?v=6AuG8itczN8

Watch Young Simba and adult Simba from the London cast talk about the connection they must maintain throughout the show.

The Lion King: The Stampede (movie)

https://www.youtube.com/watch?v=5IFLz4CETj4

Check out the amazing 2.5 minutes that took over two years to make. Now, how would you recreate this on stage?

#LiveatFive with Jelani Remy of *The Lion King*

http://www.broadway.com/videos/157967/broadwaycom-liveatfive-with-jelani-remy-of-the-lion-king

Meet Jelani Remy and learn how he went from being "the back legs of the rhino" in 2009 in a Las Vegas production to playing Simba on Broadway starting in 2015.

360° Video of "Circle of Life"

https://www.youtube.com/watch?v=7T57kzGQGto

Experience the opening of the Broadway show with the "Circle of Life" in 360°.

360° Video of Rehearsal

https://www.facebook.com/TheLionKingUSA/videos/10156221518772580

Watch the Broadway cast rehearse the "Lioness Hunt Dance" with this interactive video.

BOOKS

Blumenthal, Eileen, and Julie Taymor. *Julie Taymor, Playing with Fire: Theater, Opera, Film.* New York: Harry N. Abrams, Inc., 1999.

Rodosthenous, George, *Ed. The Disney Musical on Stage and Screen: Critical Approaches from "Snow White" to "Frozen."* New York: Bloomsbury Methuen Drama, 2017.

Viertel, Jack. *The Secret Life of the American Musical: How Broadway Shows are Built.* New York: Farrar, Straus and Giroux, 2016.

Wienir, David, and Jodie Langel. *Making It on Broadway: Actors' Tales of Climbing to the Top.* New York: Allworth Press, 2004.

ONLINE ARTICLES

Begley, Sarah. "Julie Taymor on *The Lion King* and Her Creative Process." *Time,* October 8, 2015. http://time.com/4065287/julie-taymor-creative-process.

Brantley, Ben. "Theater Review: Cub Comes of Age: A Twice-Told Cosmic Tale." *New York Times,* November 14, 1997. http://www.nytimes.com/1997/11/14/movies/theater-review-cub-comes-of-age-a-twice-told-cosmic-tale.html.

"Broadway: *The Lion King*." PBS.org, accessed August 11, 2017. http://www.pbs.org/wnet/broadway/shows/the-lion-king.

BWW News Desk. "Disney's *The Lion King* Tour Breaks Box Office Records in Greenville." BroadwayWorld. com, June 27, 2017. http://www.broadwayworld.com/ national-tours/article/Disneys-THE-LION-KING-Tour-Breaks-Box-Office-Records-in-Greenville-20170627.

_____. "*The Lion King* Breaks Records on Broadway & the Road." BroadwayWorld.com, December 28, 2015. https://www.broadwayworld. com/national-tours/article/THE-LION-KING-Breaks-Records-on-Broadway-the-Road-20151228.

Canby, Vincent. "Sunday View: 'The Lion King' Earns Its Roars of Approval." *New York Times*, November 23, 1997. http://www.nytimes.com/1997/11/23/theater/sunday-view-the-lion-king-earns-its-roars-of-approval.html.

Conrad, Peter. "This lioness could change your life." *Guardian*, October 2, 1999. https://www.theguardian. com/theobserver/1999/oct/03/featuresreview.review6.

Cox, Gordon. "Broadway 'Lion King' roars louder." *Variety*, February 1, 2013. http://variety.com/2013/legit/news/ broadway-lion-king-roars-louder-1118065538.

"The Demographics of the Broadway Audience 2015–2016 Season." BroadwayLeague.com. https://www. broadwayleague.com/research/research-reports.

"FAQ for *The Lion King* (1994)." IMDB.com, accessed August 7, 2017. http://www.imdb.com/title/tt0110357/faq.

Fierberg, Ruthie. "9 Secrets Director Julie Taymor Revealed about *The Lion King*." *Playbill*, January 27, 2017. http://www.playbill.com/article/9-secrets-director-julie-taymor-revealed-about-her-lion-king.

Gerard, Jeremy. "Hakuna Matata, Baby: Disney Claims Record $6.2 Billion Gross for *Lion King*." Deadline Hollywood, September 22, 2014. http://deadline.com/2014/09/disney-lion-king-highest-grossing-show-at-6-2-billion-838482.

Gilbert, Ryan. "Disney's *The Lion* King Will Unveil Newly-Configured Touring Production in October 2017." Broadway.com, September 30, 2016. http://www.broadway.com/buzz/186192/disneys-the-lion-king-will-unveil-newly-configured-touring-production-in-october-2017.

Gill, Raymond. "Reaching the Disney Heights of Design." *Sydney Morning Herald*, March 5, 2003. http://www.smh.com.au/articles/2003/03/04/1046540187705.html.

Golembewski, Vanessa. "The Secret Rivalry Between *Pocahontas* & *The Lion King*." Refinery29, June 23, 2015. http://www.refinery29.com/2015/06/89430/pocohantas-disney-anniversary-animation-team-rivalry.

Hofler, Robert. "Turning in early on B'way." *Variety*, September 15, 2002. http://variety.com/2002/legit/news/turning-in-early-on-b-way-1117872766.

Hofmeister, Sallie. "In the Realm of Marketing, *The Lion King* Rules." *New York Times*, July 12, 1994. http://www.nytimes.com/1994/07/12/business/in-the-realm-of-marketing-the-lion-king-rules.html?mcubz=1.

Hollywood Reporter staff. "'The Lion King': THR's 1994 Review." HollywoodReporter.com, June 27, 2016.

http://www.hollywoodreporter.com/review/lion-king-thrs-1994-review-906559.

"How Disney Conquered the Great White Way." NYTIX.com, accessed August 10, 2017. http://www.nytix.com/Links/Broadway/Articles/disneyonbroadway.html.

Jones, Chris. "'The Lion King': Broadway smash hit keeps rolling along." *Chicago Tribune,* December 6, 2015. http://www.chicagotribune.com/entertainment/theater/reviews/ct-lion-king-chicago-review-ent-1207-20151206-column.html.

Kane, Jessica. "Celebrities with Broadway Beginnings May Surprise You." Huffington Post, August 29, 2013. http://www.huffingtonpost.com/2013/08/29/celebrities-broadway_n_3833098.html.

Kuchwara, Michael. "One woman stands behind Broadway's best." Associated Press, August 21, 2005. http://www.nbcnews.com/id/8974469/ns/business-us_business/t/one-woman-stands-behind-broadways-best/#.WZIWmFV96Co.

Lawson, Mark. "Lion King director Julie Taymor: 'When women fail, they don't get another chance as easily'" *Guardian,* June 19, 2015. https://www.theguardian.com/stage/2015/jun/19/lion-king-director-julie-taymor-women-opportunity.

Lowenstein, Roger. "Eisner: From Corporate Savior to Bad Example." *Los Angeles Times.* February 12, 2004. http://articles.latimes.com/2004/feb/12/news/OE-LOWENSTEIN.

Maslon, Laurence. "Resurrection of 42nd Street." PBS.org, accessed August 11, 2017. http://www.pbs.org/wnet/broadway/essays/resurrection-of-42nd-street.

Moynihan, Tim. "*The Lion King* Musical in VR is an Incredible Experience." *Wired,* November 18, 2015. https://www.wired.com/2015/11/lion-king-vr-video.

Peterson, Kyle. "Disney Fans First, Then the Highbrows: How Schneider's Marketing Helped *Lion* Become King of Broadway. *Advertising Age,* February 1, 1999. http://adage.com/article/news/disney-fans-highbrows-schneider-s-marketing-helped-lion-king-broadway/63666.

Qin, Amy. "Can you say 'Hakuna Matata' in Mandarin?" *New York Times,* June 17, 2016. https://www.nytimes.com/2016/06/18/theater/the-lion-king-disneyland-shanghai.html.

Rickwald, Bethany. "Experience 'The Circle of Life' with a 360° Immersive Video from Broadway's *The Lion King.*" *TheaterMania,* November 18, 2015. http://www.theatermania.com/broadway/news/lion-king-circle-of-life-immersive-360-video_75023.html.

Robertson, Campbell. "Broadway, the Land of the Long-Running Sure Thing." *New York Times,* September 10, 2006. http://www.nytimes.com/2006/09/10/theater/broadway-the-land-of-the-longrunning-sure-thing.html.

Stanton, Angie. "BWW Interview: A Glimpse into the Wardrobe Bunker at The Lion King." Broadway World, May 19, 2016. *https://www.broadwayworld.com/national-tours/article/BWW-Interview-A-Glimpse-into-the-Wardrobe-Bunker-at-THE-LION-KING-20160519.*

Stewart, James B. "Broadway Tickets, for the Price of an Economics Lesson." *New York Times,* June 8, 2017. https://www.nytimes.com/2017/06/08/business/broadway-theater-ticket-prices.html?mcubz=1&_r=0.

Viswanathan, Vidya. "Making Theater Autism-Friendly." *Atlantic,* April 6, 2015. https://www.theatlantic.com/health/archive/2015/04/making-theater-autism-friendly/388348.

VIDEOS
"Disney's *The Lion King* Classroom Education Series" (in 10 parts). Posted June 4, 2010. https://www.youtube.com/watch?v=Couk1312hN0&list=PL749105D50D29325E

"*The Lion King:* The Making of a Walt Disney Masterpiece" (in two parts). Posted June 13, 2011. https://www.youtube.com/watch?v=WmcJthJmF98&t=89s

WEBSITES
"About The Lion King." The Walt Disney Company. http://www.lionking.com/about

"Disney's The Lion King Jr." Music Theatre International. http://www.mtishows.com/disneys-the-lion-king-jr

"*The Lion King* Study Guide." Disney Theatrical Productions Education Department. media.disneyonbroadway.com/pdf/TheLionKingStudyGuide.pdf

REPORTS
The Walt Disney Company, 1997 *Annual Report,* November 1997. http://ddd.uab.cat/pub/decmed/46860/iaDISNEYa1997ieng.pdf.

The Walt Disney Company, *Fiscal Year 2016 Annual Financial Report,* October 2016. https://ditm-twdc-us.storage.googleapis.com/2016-Annual-Report.pdf.

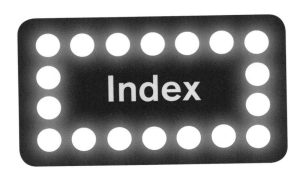

Index

Page numbers in **boldface** are illustrations.

About the Author

NANCY CAPACCIO is an actor, writer, and marketing consultant specializing in educational publishing. She has had leading roles in several stage plays as well as in a feature-length independent movie. Most of her theatrical work has been in performing and teaching Playback Theatre, a form of improvisation dedicated to helping people share their stories. Nancy has also spent years entertaining hospitalized children as "Lady Gwendolyn."

LONGWOOD PUBLIC LIBRARY
800 Middle Country Road
Middle Island, NY 11953
(631) 924-6400
longwoodlibrary.org

LIBRARY HOURS

Monday-Friday	9:30 a.m. - 9:00 p.m.
Saturday	9:30 a.m. - 5:00 p.m.
Sunday (Sept-June)	1:00 p.m. - 5:00 p.m.